W9-AVR-597

PETERSON'S
HAPPY HOUR

PETERSON'S
HAPPY HOUR

SPIRITED COCKTAILS AND HELPFUL HINTS TO BRIGHTEN DAILY LIFE

VALERIE PETERSON

CLARKSON POTTER/PUBLISHERS

NEW YORK

Additional Credits and Acknowledgments are on page 121.

Copyright © 2010 by Valerie Peterson
Ephemera photographs by Paul D'Innocenzo

All rights reserved.
Published in the United States by Clarkson Potter/Publishers,
an imprint of the Crown Publishing Group, a division of
Random House, Inc., New York.
www.crownpublishing.com
www.clarksonpotter.com

CLARKSON POTTER is a trademark and POTTER with colophon is a
registered trademark of Random House, Inc.

Library of Congress Cataloging-in-Publication Data
Peterson, Valerie.
Peterson's happy hour: spirited cocktails and helpful hints for
year-round cheer / Valerie Peterson. —1st ed.
        p.   cm.
Includes index.
1. Cocktails.   I. Title.   II. Title: Happy hour.
TX951.P4854   2010
641.8'74—dc22   2009030135

ISBN 978-0-307-59051-0

Printed in China

Design by Stephanie Huntwork

1   3   5   7   9   10   8   6   4   2

First Edition

To the folks of Clunie Avenue in Yonkers,
past & present,
especially
Edie & Harry Firstenberg

With thanks for the memories and love

CONTENTS

INTRODUCTION
IS YOUR DAILY GRIND BEGINNING TO GRATE? SMOOTH THE ROUGH EDGES WITH A HAPPY HOUR.

My days were once like yours. Entrenched in e-mail and Twitter and Facebook and YouTube, my overtaxed mind didn't have a lot of time to spend on the issues that affect our world. Befuddled by byzantine HMO "out of network" paperwork, confused by recycling-bin strictures, flummoxed by the plot of *LOST,* I had nary a brain cell left for more important things. After all, how could I worry about The Big Picture when my sanity was threatened by endless loops of computerized customer-service "help" lines, appliances that failed a day after their warranties were up, that persistent man from the collection agency . . . Something had to give.

A battery of self-help books informed me that if I couldn't change my line of credit, I could at least change the line on the bottom of my face. But how? How to achieve the serenity enjoyed in days of yore while living in this fast-paced, vexatious modern world?

After spending hours poring over authoritative historic documentation (i.e., watching *The Thin Man* on DVD and looking at other people's photo albums), I realized that the adult smiles of "simpler times" were very often accompanied by an amazing substance with the ability to transform—that the solution to petty nuisances literally had been in front of me all along: liquor.

Yes, the key to happier hours is . . . a happy hour! Like the ringing of the Good Humor Man's bell to children, the cry quickens the adult heart and brings with it the promise of a convivial experience, a treat for the palate, and cool relief from the hot mess of the day.

Happy Hours have helped me, and they can help you, too.

So when snafus are making you snappish, when minor irritations are giving you a case of the shingles, when slight interpersonal frictions threaten to ignite into full-blown fireballs, *Peterson's Happy Hour* has the liquid antidotes.

A refreshing tequila tonic can cool you during a computer meltdown. An orange-infused, sparkling cocktail can dull the recollection of that unfortunate babysitting mishap. And a fanciful 'tini at quitting time can make you forget that slight accounting boo-boo— at least until the FTC notices. Yes, taken in moderation, the tasty elixirs described herein will boost your mood and brighten your outlook . . . and help you put that bedbug infestation into perspective.

This book is organized by common daily frustrations and provides the refreshing cocktail relief for each. Sidebars offer sage advice on related topics, and the back of the book is chock-full of handy information and can guide you to the appropriate drink for your particular Happy-Hour need, whether it be a tasty vodka tipple for one or a rum punch for a festive crowd.

In fact, all of *Peterson's* concoctions are most effective when enjoyed with friends, and most satisfying when consumed responsibly (see Insurance Policy on page 11 for further details).

War, pestilence, the economy, the environment: *Peterson's* doesn't presume to be able to solve all of the world's ills.

But sometimes, when the day hands you lemons, a shot of limoncello can help you brush off minor annoyances. And really, once you've figured out how to breeze through the little irritations, can fostering world peace be very far behind?

A NOTE ON THE RECIPES

THESE RECIPES taste most delicious when you use the best ingredients available—like freshly squeezed juices (especially for your lemon juice and lime juice), fruits in season, and good-quality liquors. When soft drinks (like cola, lemon-lime soda, tonic water, or ginger ale) are called for, *Peterson's* recommends the all-natural options that are now widely available. A few of the recipes call for homemade infused vodkas and simple syrups—rest assured, they're very, very easy to make.

Note that it's optional but nice to put a chill on your glassware and, to ensure there are no off tastes to mar your concoctions, it's best to use filtered water in your ades and in your ice. See Glassware (page 119) and Ice, Ice Baby (page 115) for more helpful information.

Of course, your days are tough enough without stressing about your cocktail ingredients, so improvise as you see fit, with *Peterson's* blessing.

HAPPY HOURS are cheeriest when timed appropriately— that is, *after* work and the day's chores are finished, when heavy thinking and/ or heavy lifting is no longer required. Therefore, despite the obvious appeal of sip- ping a tension-reducing cocktail *while* you are in the throes of a tussle with the Excel spreadsheet/ customer-service desk/your mother, it is crucial to hold off until the annual budget/refund/ armistice is ironed out. And while a little buzz can be good, it's defi- nitely not advisable when using, say, a chain saw or operating any other equipment with sharp edges, wheels, or other moving parts.

So, while enjoying the refreshments described within, put safety first and do not get in your car, attempt to fix your roof, or decide it's a good time to "finally do something" about the neigh- bors' disgraceful hedges. And if you're expecting, experts caution against imbibing until the baby is born, so stick with the mocktails. But there's a bright side to that: It gives you a reason to look for- ward to labor.

INTERPERSONAL
POTIONS
1

AMID THE TRIALS OF DAILY LIFE, YOU'RE GRATEFUL for the friends and family, neighbors and colleagues who surround you. Like any tribe, your community offers protection, security, affection—and even health. Scientific studies suggest that a supportive social network is one of the secrets to longevity—after all, where would *you* be without the sympathetic ear of your beloved spouse/pastor/hairdresser?

Yes, those closest are there for you in times of joy and celebration, in times of need and sorrow. Unfortunately, they're also there when you want to watch your favorite television show without being talked at. When you don't need to hear that you should work on your peanut-butter-cup/two-pack-a-day/scratch-off-lottery-ticket addiction. When you would rather *not* be reminded that your new haircut makes you look "just like Kate Gosselin."

Yes, sometimes the gift of companionship is wrapped in loud snoring—that is, the bonds of society come at a price. In order to get free babysitting, you have to accept unwanted child-rearing advice. In order to get a hand with fixing your lawn mower, you have to listen to instructions on the *right* way to sod. In order to get fixed up with the hot cousin-of-a-friend, you have to submit to suggestions for a head-to-toe makeover.

But really, you wouldn't trade those close to you for anything. So when, despite all good intentions, heck is other people, keep the interpersonal from getting incendiary with a cocktail: a pacifying potion that can help prevent your being smothered in the bosom of humanity.

SHANDY RELATIONS

YOU TWO are so completely different, it's hard to believe you share the same bloodlines. You love the hustle and bustle of the city; he needs to be ten miles from civilization. You revel in your high-profile desk job; he works the land. No, you don't have much in common. But when he expertly taps that keg for the beer-and-limeade shandys . . . well, there's no mistaking the family resemblance.

SERVES 1

6 ounces (¾ cup) ice-cold beer

6 ounces (¾ cup) prepared Limeade (see below)

Pour the beer, then the limeade, into a chilled pilsner glass.

Try
Gretz
Beer

LIMEADE (OR LEMONADE) SERVES 6

2 cups (16 ounces) fresh lime (or lemon) juice

1 cup (8 ounces) simple syrup (page 112), or to taste

3 cups (24 ounces) cold water (you can substitute chilled club soda to make it fizzy)

Combine the lime juice and simple syrup. Add the water and mix thoroughly. Add more simple syrup, to taste, if desired.

JUL 58

BEACH-HOUSE BOGART

WHEN YOU agreed to share a summerhouse, you hadn't realized the others would be so inconsiderate. Everyone leaves their dirty dishes around the kitchen and you've spent half your time labeling your provisions so nobody else will take them. . . . Hmmm, looks like someone bought your favorite brand of sour-apple liqueur. Surely they won't miss a cup or so for your famous double-apple gelatin shots? You, of course, will be sure to hide *your* liquor bottles where they'll never find them: under the sink, behind the dishwashing liquid.

SERVES 12

- 1 envelope unflavored gelatin
- 1 cup apple juice
- 1 cup sour-apple liqueur
- 2 ounces (4 table-spoons) fresh lime juice

Sprinkle the gelatin over ¼ cup of the apple juice in a bowl or a large measuring cup with a spout. While the gelatin softens, put the remaining ¾ cup of the apple juice in a small saucepan and bring to a boil over high heat. Pour the boiling apple juice over the gelatin–apple juice mixture and stir to dissolve the gelatin completely. Add the sour-apple liqueur and lime juice. Divide the mixture into twelve 2-ounce gelatin-shot cups (see Resources, page 120). Set the cups on a tray or shallow pan (for ease of refrigeration) and place in the refrigerator until set (allow at least 2 hours).

SECURITY BLANKET

THE NEW guy next door seems a tad overzealous in his neighborhood-watch duties. True, the high-schoolers aren't pulling any more late-night shenanigans and the rodent population is down. But the paperboy is too terrified to deliver and the mail carrier is "accidentally" leaving your correspondence at a house around the corner. Perhaps you should offer Mr. Home-block Security a calming rum nightcap and tell him you'll take tonight's shift.

SERVES 1

2 ounces dark rum

1 ounce (2 table-spoons) honey

6 ounces (¾ cup) hot milk

freshly grated nutmeg, for garnish

Mix the rum and honey in a mug. Add the milk and stir until the honey melts and all the ingredients are well combined. Grate nutmeg on top.

BABY BLANKET SERVES 1

1 ounce (2 tablespoons) honey

6 ounces (¾ cup) hot milk

scant ¼ teaspoon vanilla extract

freshly grated nutmeg, for garnish

Place honey in a mug. Microwave for 15–20 seconds to heat (this will make honey easier to mix). Add the hot milk and vanilla extract and stir to mix. Grate nutmeg on top.

MODERN DATING TIPS

With today's electronic shortcuts to meeting romantic partners, it's easy to forget that intimacy is a gradual process and shouldn't be rushed. Proceed with caution if, early in the relationship, your new paramour:

- insists on becoming more physical than you are comfortable with.

- is a little too enthusiastic when he tells you how much you remind him of his mother.

- asks you to name him/her a beneficiary of your life-insurance policy.

FUZZY DATE

HIS PROFILE said "young at heart" and "likes to cuddle"—obviously, there is some kind of coded language to this Internet-dating thing. While you rethink your online-screening methods, snuggle up with a peachy, thoroughly adult cocktail, stuffed date optional.

SERVES 1

3 tablespoons Date-Orange Puree (page 113)

1 ounce Drambuie

1 ounce peach schnapps

3 dashes peach bitters (such as Fee's)

pitted date, for garnish

dried apricot sliver, for garnish

Pour the puree, Drambuie, peach schnapps, and peach bitters into a cocktail shaker filled with ice. Shake well (until condensation forms on the entire shaker). Strain the mixture into a chilled cocktail glass. Stuff the date with the sliver of dried apricot, then skewer the apricot-stuffed date on a decorative pick and rest on the rim of the glass.

AUNTIE DOTE

THE LAST thing you remember, your precious charges were offering you some liquid refreshment. Obviously, the Bad Seeds take after their mother. You have to admit, the bubbly cocktails tasted good going down, but it's going to be a while before you agree to babysit again. And only if the kids tell you what was in the drink.

SERVES 1

1½ ounces B&B (Benedictine & Brandy)

¾ ounce orange liqueur (such as triple sec)

5 ounces champagne or sparkling wine

Pour the B&B and orange liqueur into a champagne flute. Add the champagne.

BABYSITTING NO-NO'S

Your day has been frantic—and you just need a free minute to run into the drugstore/pop into the shower/call the astrology hotline. But although modern conveniences *seem* to afford ingenious ways to briefly contain the little ones while you're otherwise occupied, note that the following methods are frowned upon by parenting experts and/or law-enforcement officials:

- Plopping child in front of an "electronic babysitter," such as television, a game console, or a slot machine
- Locking him/her in the car without adult supervision
- Tethering kiddy "leash" to parking meter outside a store
- Administering tranquilizing dosages of "Mommy's medicine"
- Using a Taser

JAN • 63 •

PET PEEVE
(Strawberry Caipirinha)

WHEN YOU bargained the kids down from a rottweiler puppy to a tropical bird, you thought, "A little birdseed, a little newspaper, and it will all be so easy." But the only word he's learned is *cachaça* and he's figured out how to open his cage door. Hmmm, you wonder if he can be trained to use the cocktail muddler.

SERVES 1

½ lime, cut into 4 wedges

2 large or 3 medium fresh strawberries, rinsed, hulled, and sliced in half (see Note), plus one whole strawberry for garnish

1 tablespoon muscovado sugar (or substitute dark-brown sugar)

2 ounces cachaça

Put the lime wedges and strawberry halves in a rocks glass. Add the sugar and, using a muddler or wooden spoon, muddle the fruit with the sugar until the fruit releases all its juices and the sugar is dissolved. Add ice to the glass and pour the cachaça over all. Gently stir. Skewer the strawberry on a decorative pick and place in the glass.

NOTE: You can substitute frozen strawberries for muddling, but thaw first.

MUSCLE RELAXANT

YOU'VE WAITED a half hour to get into the yoga studio—and then you were nearly trampled in the rush for floor space. The woman next to you flings sweat with every change in pose and Mr. Commando's downward dogs are smack in your line of sight. After ninety minutes of personal space invasions—never mind the contortionist poses—you need something to calm your frazzled nerves—maybe an Eastern-influenced lemongrass, ginger, and pineapple cocktail. Ah, *namaste*!

SERVES 1

2 ounces Ginger-Lemongrass-Infused Vodka (page 114)

2 ounces pineapple juice

½ ounce (1 tablespoon) fresh lime juice

2 pineapple chunks, for garnish

Pour the vodka, pineapple juice, and lime juice into a cocktail shaker filled with ice. Shake well (until condensation forms on the entire shaker). Pour into a chilled cocktail glass. Garnish with the pineapple skewered onto a cocktail pick.

ZEN AND THE ART OF HOGGING FLOOR SPACE

It can be hard to find breathing room in a popular yoga class. Try these hints to help clear the deck.

- Subtly create an eighteen-inch perimeter around your mat with your blocks, water bottle, towel, etc.

- Immediately sit on your mat and feign a deep, meditative trance.

- If someone asks you to scooch over or to squish in, look at them blankly and say, *"Como?"*

- Talk loudly about your previous night's dinner of five-bean chili.

- Don't bathe for three days before class.

BOOK-CLUB RULES

Forming a book club is an excellent way to ensure ongoing intellectual stimulation. Many such groups thrive for decades and long-lived clubs show remarkable similarities in the way they are conducted. To follow the lead of these flourishing clubs, adopt the following rules, which have proven successful in maintaining interpersonal harmony as well as lively discussion:

- Read less-expensive paperback editions.
- When voting on selections, majority rules.
- Members must take turns hosting.
- Be respectful of others' opinions, even if they differ from your own!
- Insist on a two-drink minimum.

BOOK-CLUB BUCK

THANKFULLY, your husband didn't notice your new designer purse. And when he asked what "the girls" were reading this week, you pulled the "Edgar Allan Poe" card out of your sleeve. You were inspired, of course, by the Amontillado-based buck served at the last, ah, "discussion." It's good you've been getting a lot of practice bluffing—because what happens at Book Club, stays at Book Club.

SERVES 1

2 ounces Amontillado sherry

1 ounce Ginger-Lime-Infused Simple Syrup (page 112)

½ ounce (1 tablespoon) fresh lime juice

2 to 3 ounces club soda

curl of lime peel, for garnish

Pour the sherry, simple syrup, and lime juice into a cocktail shaker filled with ice. Shake well (until condensation forms on the entire shaker). Strain the mixture into a rocks glass filled with ice. Top with the club soda. Place the lime peel in the glass.

ST. KIR

YOUR RELATIVES are incessantly bragging about your Goody-Two-Shoes cousin, who always manages to make you look like a troublemaker. You were afraid she'd put a damper on your pre-wedding festivities, until you found out her weakness—those sparkling elderflower-and-blackcurrant cocktails that are as heavenly as they are sinful. Serve her a couple at the bridal shower—and if she's half as raucous as she was at the bachelor-ette party, the aunts and uncles will be gossiping for months.

SERVES 1

½ ounce St-Germain elderflower liqueur

½ ounce crème de cassis (black-currant liqueur)

5 ounces sparkling wine (such as prosecco or cava), well chilled

thin curl of orange peel, for garnish

Combine the elderflower liqueur and crème de cassis in a champagne flute. Add the sparkling wine. Hang the orange peel on the rim of the glass.

BRIDAL SHOWER SIGNALS

Those "off-the-registry" offerings may be sending a subtle message about the true feelings of the giver. Learn from the following examples and you, too, will be able to interpret the wedding-shower stash:

POULTRY SHEARS FROM GRANDMAMA:

"You are lazy if you buy your chicken already cut into parts. But I don't judge."

IRON AND IRONING BOARD FROM AUNT MARTHA:

"Yes, that's what marriage is all about. . . . Get used to it."

alternately

"It's obvious that, despite your being thirty-two years old, you don't own one."

NAUGHTY NIGHTIE FROM THE SISTER-IN-LAW:

"I should be so lucky."

WINE-OF-THE-MONTH CLUB FROM THE MAID OF HONOR:

"I want to give you every chance of being happy together!"

2 WORKDAY UNWINDERS

IT'S THURSDAY, YOU'VE ALREADY PUT IN FIFTY hours this week, and the new Senior Vice President, Corporate Economies, still expects you to finish that twenty-page report on how to more efficiently organize future reports. You've been asked to use the backs of previously printed paper because nobody can afford to waste paper in the midst of the economic crisis/global-warming crisis/executive-bonus crisis. You'll have to get it done tonight because tomorrow you're attending an all-day meeting to discuss how to more efficiently plan future meetings. After all, nobody can afford to waste time and energy in this world of wildly fluctuating department budgets/stock prices/executive bonuses.

Welcome to work, twenty-first-century style! Dwindling resources mean cutbacks on those most important things: conference-room birthday cakes; ergonomically correct "status" chairs; free coffee. Yes, you know that "employment" is the new "promotion"—but it would be easier to be grateful for the job if you weren't forced to endure cost-saving measures like reduced benefits/revocation of personal-bathroom keys/"Legume Week" in the cafeteria.

Worse, dwindling staffs mean there's more . . . *work*. The powers-that-be seem to have laid off anyone who knows anything about how to write a requisition form/code the budget sheets/operate the tele-conferencing equipment, and the Senior Vice President, Corporate Economies, requires all of those things. Without adequate staffing, your office days have gotten longer and yet there's barely time to be civil to your coworkers/use the bathroom/do your online comparison shopping.

Happily, one thing that hasn't changed is your regular night out with the gang. Of course, after the company-wide pay cuts, all you can afford to order now are the two-dollar beer specials. In fact, the only one who can spring for fancy cocktails is the Senior Vice President, Corporate Economies. Luckily for you and your coworkers, it's still economical to make a stiff drink at home.

PINK SLIP-PER SANGRIA

PERHAPS YOU could've been a bit more diplomatic in the e-mail and referred to your boss as "detail-oriented" rather than "a %$#@*! control freak." And you *were* a little quick with the Send button; you would have preferred to not have actually copied him on the correspondence. Fire off a pitcher of this dry, fruity, pink sangria and invite your colleagues over—so you can practice your apology while waiting for the other shoe to drop.

SERVES 8–10

1 orange, unpeeled, washed, and cut into ½-inch chunks

1 large, ripe peach, washed and cut into ½-inch chunks

1 pint (2 cups) fresh strawberries, washed, hulled, and sliced

1 cup (8 ounces) brandy

one 750 ml. bottle rosé wine, well chilled

2 cups (16 ounces) club soda, well chilled

Put the fruit and brandy into a pitcher and mix them thoroughly, then leave the mixture to macerate for at least 2 hours, preferably overnight in the refrigerator. When ready to serve, add the chilled rosé and then the chilled club soda. Add a bit of fruit to each glass before serving.

GREEN DAZE

YOU DIDN'T mind when they asked you to bring your own mug to work or when they substituted hand dryers for paper towels. You've dutifully relabeled and reused file folders and you didn't even make a fuss when they changed to one-ply in the bathroom. But when they suggested you reuse your tea bags, they went too far. Go home and brew this tea-rific green Chartreuse cocktail. And use the whole tea bag—it's worth the sacrifice to Mother Earth.

SERVES 1

turbinado sugar, for rimming

1½ ounces Chartreuse liqueur, plus extra for rimming

1½ ounces (6 tablespoons) brewed green tea, well chilled

¾ ounce (1½ tablespoons) fresh lime juice

3 dashes peach bitters (such as Fee's)

kiwi slice, for garnish

Place the sugar in a saucer slightly larger in diameter than the rim of the glass. Pour some Chartreuse in another saucer. Dip the rim of a cocktail glass first in the Chartreuse, then in the sugar. Allow to dry. Combine the green tea, Chartreuse, lime juice, and peach bitters in a cocktail shaker filled with ice. Shake well (until condensation forms on the entire shaker). Strain into the rimmed cocktail glass. Cut the kiwi slice halfway through and hang it on the rim of the glass.

What every young girl should know

AMERICANS drink more coffee than any other beverage except water.

They drink it first of all because they like it. But most people only vaguely realize that coffee sharpens the mind, improves reason and judgment and self-control, physical strength and accuracy of movements. These facts are all found in medical literature. And if you are like 97 out of a hundred people, you don't need worry about sleeping, for the lift you get from coffee lasts only two hours.

So what every young girl ought to know, if she hopes some day to be a good wife, is how to make good coffee — morning, noon and night.

And the rules are simple: Use a heaping tablespoonful for every cup, and keep your utensils clean!

Coffee perks you up!

Published by the Pan American coffee producers, for the benefit of the American public, the largest consumers of coffee in the world.

BRAZIL · COLOMBIA · COSTA RICA · CUBA · EL SALVADOR · VENEZUELA

Pan American Coffee Bureau
New York City

ADULTERATED COFFEE BREAK

YOU'VE BEEN looking forward to a twenty-minute breather but, once again, there are no clean mugs and whoever absconded with the last cup of joe ran off without making a fresh pot. You spend most of your downtime brewing and stewing—and thinking that a little Kahlúa would make this a *real* break.

SERVES 1

1½ ounces coffee liqueur (such as Kahlúa)

6 ounces (¾ cup) strong, brewed coffee, chilled

2 ounces milk or half-and-half

½ ounce (1 tablespoon) simple syrup (page 112), or to taste (optional)

Put the coffee liqueur, chilled coffee, milk, and simple syrup (if using) into a shaker filled with ice. Shake well (until condensation forms on the entire shaker). Pour the mixture into a highball glass filled with ice.

NO COMPANY PICNIC

(aka Watermelon Mojito)

THE MEMO regarding the dress code was longer than your employment contract and your supervisor has dropped ominous hints that "the big boss" doesn't want to be beaten in the sack race. As a result, the company's "casual summer outing" is about as relaxing as an I.R.S. audit. There's one improvement upon the other picnics you've been to, however: Your watermelon has no pits and includes rum.

SERVES 6

¼ large watermelon, to yield 6 cups watermelon puree

1 cup mint leaves, well washed and loosely packed, plus 6 sprigs for garnish

¼ cup sugar

¾ cup (6 ounces) fresh lime juice

1½ cups (12 ounces) white rum

Remove the seeds from the watermelon and cut the fruit into chunks, approximately 1½ inches square. Using a cocktail muddler or a wooden spoon, muddle (i.e., crush) the mint with the sugar in a 3-quart pitcher until mint is bruised. Add the lime juice and rum. Puree the watermelon chunks in the blender and add to the mixture in the pitcher. Stir to mix thoroughly.

To serve, fill each highball glass halfway with crushed ice. Add the mojito mixture to the glasses and place a mint sprig in each glass.

MIGHTY I.T.

Computer acting up in the middle of your workday? Given the complex technical issues involved with repairing these incredibly sensitive machines, it's best that you leave their care to the highly trained experts. Here's what they suggest:

"Turn it off, unplug it, plug it in, turn it on again." —P.C. Tech

"Turn it off, unplug it, plug it in, turn it on again, dude."
  —Mac Genius

TECH TONIC

BETWEEN YOUR Internet dating and your social networking, you suspect you may have overloaded your computer's memory. Well, at least you have a valid excuse for your boss about why you're late with the budget spreadsheet. Put in the call to I.T.—then you might as well leave early for a tech-ila cocktail. Sometimes you think life with computers isn't all it's cracked up to be. But then again, you can't Google your ex-boyfriends with the *Encyclopedia Britannica,* can you?

SERVES 1

2 ounces tequila

1 ounce (2 table-spoons) fresh lime juice

3 dashes orange bitters (such as Fee's)

4 ounces (½ cup) tonic water

lime slice, for garnish

Combine the tequila, lime juice, and bitters in a cocktail shaker filled with ice. Shake well (until condensation forms on the entire shaker). Strain the mixture into a highball glass ¾ filled with ice. Top with the tonic water. Cut the lime slice halfway through and hang it on the side of the glass.

HOLE PUNCH

THEY'VE ELIMINATED your favorite medium-nib pen from the "approved" list and the Supplies Czar—aka the office manager—called you on the carpet regarding your profligate use of sticky notes. Luckily, your home stationery drawer is as well stocked as your liquor cabinet. The chill of this whiskey-pear-ginger punch is reinforced with an ice ring; mix up a batch for the office party and label yourself smart for squirreling away those staples *before* the penny-pinching.

SERVES 14

2 cups (16 ounces) blended whiskey

1 quart pear nectar, well chilled

one 750 ml. bottle vinho verde wine, well chilled

1 liter ginger ale, preferably all-natural, well chilled

pear Ice Ring (page 117)

Combine all the ingredients in a punch bowl. Add the ice ring. Ladle into punch cups to serve.

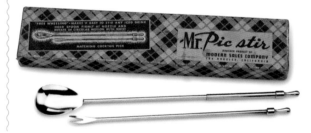

DOWNSIZING ETIQUETTE

When expressing your concern to a colleague who has recently been made redundant, take care to avoid potentially sensitive topics that might inadvertently remind him/her of the full extent of the job loss:

"Subsidized/schmubsidized, you won't miss the lousy cafeteria food."

"That company car never *was* your best color."

"You're leaving just in time—the bonus situation is going to be bleak this year."

"Do you mind if I put my name on your chair before someone else claims it? Those ergonomic babies are hard to come by these days."

GOLF-COURSE ETIQUETTE

While golf can be a frustrating game for beginners, it is best to not show too much negative emotion on the course. Avoid such unfortunate displays as:

- using foul language.
- hacking at trees, bushes, or the green.
- throwing your club.
- backing the cart over any member of your foursome.

THE HANDICAP

YOUR NEW boss thought it was a good idea to close the big sale over eighteen holes and lunch at his club. It's been a while since you played, but considering the huge size of the course and its lack of windmills, you don't feel you're doing too badly—so you don't understand why the rest of the foursome keep making snide remarks. Perhaps they're just jealous that you're not waiting until the halfway house to sip the vodka refresher you brought. What's the problem? It's not like you're driving the cart.

SERVES 8

3 cups (24 ounces) prepared iced tea, well chilled

3 cups (24 ounces) prepared lemonade, well chilled

2 cups (16 ounces) Lemon-Infused Vodka, homemade (page 115) or store-bought

8 thin lemon wedges, for garnish

Combine all the ingredients in a pitcher. Pour into collins glasses filled with ice. Skewer the lemon wedges with unused golf tees, place in the glasses, and serve.

TRADITIONAL "ARNOLD PALMER" (NONALCOHOLIC)

Combine 1 part iced tea and 1 part lemonade in a tall glass filled with ice. Garnish with a tee-skewered lemon wedge, as above.

3 } RECREATIONAL
RESTORATIVES

REMEMBER THE DAYS WHEN LEISURE TIME USED TO be, well, *relaxing*? A respite from the job and chores, the pastimes you considered "play" were meant to refresh and restore psychic equilibrium and to tip the work/life scale back into balance. Unfortunately, downtime pursuits have stress factors all their own.

Cell phones alone have contributed much anxiety to present-day recreational endeavors. You elicit homicidal glares when you forget (again!) to turn your ringer off at the movies. Intimate details of yapping strangers' lives beleaguer your quiet moments of contemplation at the park/art museum/blackjack table. Worst of all, you can be found any time of the day or night.

Good ol'-fashioned games have their share of problems, too, both age-old and modern. Your bridge night has become fraught with intracouple squabbling. Your kid's soccer coach has just made an unfortunate surprise appearance on *20/20*. You've developed a tic from playing online poker.

Whatever your preferred activities, if the state of your play leaves something to be desired, perhaps it's time to amuse yourself with a cocktail. It's a refreshing way to recover from your relaxation.

MARATHON MANHATTAN

LUNGS BURSTING, you trudge toward the finish line with tens of thousands of similarly delusional people, including that club of show-off "Running Great-Grandmothers" who just passed you. How did you let yourself get talked into this? The worst part was your "Sober October" training. But you're nearly there—just eight more miles to the finish line. Visualize sitting in your Barcalounger sipping a painkilling draught of this cocktail classic. If you finish in less than six hours, have yourself a double.

SERVES 1 OR 2

4 ounces (½ cup) rye whiskey

2 ounces sweet vermouth

4 dashes Angostura bitters

1 or 2 maraschino cherries, for garnish

In a mixing glass (or a cocktail shaker) filled with ice, add the rye, vermouth, and bitters. Stir. Strain into a double-rocks glass filled with ice or into two chilled cocktail glasses. Garnish each drink with a cherry.

NOTE: For longest shelf life, vermouth should be stored in the refrigerator after opening.

PERFECT GIFTS FOR MOM

Of course, you're thinking that your mom really has everything she needs and that she'd rather have something *of* you—a framed picture, perhaps, or something you lovingly handcrafted yourself that she can cherish always.

Actually, she doesn't need any more dust collectors. Cough up a piece of decent jewelry—she went through *childbirth* for you, for pity's sake.

MOM-OSA

THE KIDS are making you breakfast in bed and you're trying to not think about what sounded like an explosion or that smell of burning rubber. Luckily, they've served you a pitcher of your favorite morning beverage. Before you survey the damages, fortify yourself with this sparkling, maple-orange treat. Mmmm, some things you've taught them well . . .

SERVES 5

10 ounces (1¼ cups) orange juice, well chilled

2½ ounces pasteurized liquid egg white

2½ ounces maple syrup

¼ teaspoon orange bitters (such as Fee's)

one 750 ml. bottle prosecco or cava, well chilled

5 long, thin orange peels, for garnish

Combine the orange juice, egg white, maple syrup, and bitters in a shaker with ice. Shake well (until condensation forms on the entire shaker). Strain the orange-juice mixture into a pitcher and add the prosecco. Serve immediately out of the pitcher, hanging an orange peel on each glass.

ALTERNATELY: Divide prosecco evenly among 5 champagne flutes. Strain approximately 3 ounces of orange-juice mixture into each glass and hang orange peels on them.

THE ALL-AMERICAN

BETWEEN THE tickets, the parking, the hot dogs, and the souvenirs, the baseball game cost $120 a head—and that's not counting your beer tab. But look at the bright side: If you stay home to watch the game, you can upgrade your drink. This bourbon-applejack cooler is as made-in-the-U.S.A. as the national sport . . . and it tastes as good as Mom's apple pie.

SERVES 1

1 ounce Kentucky bourbon

1 ounce apple brandy (such as Laird's Applejack)

1½ ounces apple cider, preferably unfiltered

½ ounce (1 tablespoon) lemon juice, plus extra for brushing apple garnish

apple slice, for garnish

Combine the bourbon, apple brandy, cider, and lemon juice in a cocktail shaker filled with ice. Shake well (until condensation forms on the entire shaker). Strain into a cocktail glass. Hang the apple slice on the glass for a garnish.

NOTE: Brush the apple slice with lemon juice to prevent browning.

SPARTON COSMIC EYE TELEVISION

Recommended by America's fine stores

for its Vivid Realism

The Higbee Company, Cleveland, Ohio, interprets Sparton TV realism in special display, above, in their store this week. Model shown is the beautiful 21" Sparton Carrington.

for its Quality

Sparton
cosmic eye television

Here is television performance created to the highest engineering standards . . . Sparton Cosmic Eye Television. Sparton owners get reception so steady, clear and true it's like having an eye in the sky.

Sparton makes over 70% of its own vital operating parts, performs many extra assembly steps by hand. Result: a virtually custom-built instrument that is famous for smooth, trouble-free, service-free operation.

Spartons are sold in the better stores that have a reputation for fine products and fine services. You'll find the address of your nearest Sparton dealer in the Yellow Pages of your telephone book.

SOLD IN SUCH FINE STORES AS:

John Wanamaker • • • New York, New York
The Dayton Company • Minneapolis, Minnesota
Meier & Frank Company, Inc. • Portland, Oregon
Joslin's • • • • • • • Denver, Colorado
And other quality stores across the nation

SPARTON RADIO-TELEVISION, JACKSON, MICHIGAN, SPECIALISTS IN ENGINEERING AND ELECTRONICS SINCE 1900. ALSO: SPARTON OF CANADA, LTD; SPARTON AUTOMOTIVE; STEGER FURNITURE CO.; DIVISIONS OF THE SPARKS-WITHINGTON COMPANY, JACKSON, MICHIGAN.

KID-FRIENDLY AMUSEMENT MOCKTAIL SERVES 1

2 ounces Ginger-Lime-Infused
   Simple Syrup (page 112)
½ ounce (1 tablespoon) fresh lime
   juice
6 ounces club soda
maraschino cherry, for garnish

Pour the simple syrup and the lime juice into a glass and stir to mix. Fill the glass ¾ full of ice. Add the club soda and stir gently. Top with the maraschino cherry.

THEME-PARK PRESCRIPTION

WHO SAYS the rides are just for kids? Now that you're an adult, you've got the money to go on them as many times as you want! Except the roller coaster wrenched your back, the bumper cars gave you whiplash, and the Tilt-A-Whirl has made you a little nauseous. Dull the aches and calm your stomach with a soothing, adults-only whiskey-and-ginger-lime concoction and you'll soon be ready for your corn dog and cotton candy.

SERVES 1

2 ounces blended whiskey

1 ounce Ginger–Lime–Infused Simple Syrup (page 112)

½ ounce (1 tablespoon) fresh lime juice

3 to 4 ounces club soda, well chilled

lime slice, for garnish

Pour the whiskey, simple syrup, and lime juice into a shaker filled with ice. Shake well (until condensation forms on the entire shaker). Strain into a highball glass ¾ filled with ice. Top with the club soda and stir gently. Hang the lime slice on the glass.

SPARKLE PLENTY

THE KIDS are clamoring for pyrotechnics, but the guy selling fireworks at the roadside stand is missing a few fingers. Hmmm. Perhaps it's a sign you should leave the display to the professionals and stick with a *liquid* sparkler. This berry festive beverage will light up your celebration nicely.

SERVES 1

½ ounce (1 tablespoon) Cranadine Syrup (page 114)

6 ounces sparkling white wine, such as prosecco or cava

5 or 6 fresh blueberries

Pour the syrup into the bottom of a champagne flute to create a red layer. Pour the sparkling wine into the glass. Float the blueberries on top.

NOTE: You can use frozen blueberries, thawed, but they may not float.

LI'L SPARKLER: Substitute ginger ale for the wine in the recipe.

FISH-STORY PUNCH

YOU REMEMBER it so vividly—the tension on your line—and it was on! You thought your arms would break during the life-or-death battle with nature, man vs. beast, you against the elements. Then, just when all seemed lost, you somehow found strength for that final effort and . . . got him! Relive your moment of triumph over a glass of spiced-rum punch worthy of Captain Ahab. As a matter of fact, you recollect that yours was the second-largest fish ever caught by your age group.

SERVES 1

1½ ounces spiced rum

1 ounce peach schnapps

½ ounce (1 tablespoon) fresh lemon juice

½ ounce (1 tablespoon) simple syrup (see page 112)

1 ounce (2 tablespoons) strongly brewed black tea, cooled

Combine the rum, peach schnapps, lemon juice, and simple syrup in a cocktail shaker filled with ice. Shake well (until condensation forms on the entire shaker). Strain the mixture over ice into a rocks glass. Add the tea and stir gently.

FOR A BOATLOAD OF FISH-STORY PUNCH SERVES 12

3 cups (24 ounces) spiced rum

2 cups (16 ounces) peach schnapps

1 cup (8 ounces) fresh lemon juice, well chilled

1 cup (8 ounces) simple syrup, well chilled

2 cups (16 ounces) strongly brewed black tea, cooled and well chilled

Combine all ingredients in a punch bowl. Add decorative Iceberg (page 117).

DOWNTURN LIMONCELLO

DARN THAT "correction" in the market: When you'd normally be on the Amalfi Coast, you have to make do with a folding chair and a sun reflector on the roof of your building. If your superintendent catches you, offer him a bribe—an ice-cold shot of your money-saving, homemade limoncello. You'll both feel like you're on a beach in Italy.

MAKES APPROXIMATELY 1½ QUARTS

1 liter Lemon–Infused Vodka (page 115)

2½ cups (20 ounces) simple syrup (page 112)

Combine the vodka and simple syrup in a 2-quart glass jar with an airtight lid (see Resources, page 120). Allow to sit at room temperature for one day. Store in the freezer and drink ice-cold out of shot glasses.

PINCHING PENNIES . . . AND PROVISIONS

Feeling the economic pinch? Do a good deed while stocking your home shelves at the same time: Take your Depression-era great-aunt Sadie to a diner for coffee. Listen to her stories of "the good old days," about how they scrimped and saved and walked five miles uphill both to and from school while you watch her stash paper napkins, packets of sugar, bathroom tissue, etc., in her bag. When you're done, offer to pay for her cup of joe— *if* she splits the goods with you.

BUG ZAPPER

THE MOTHER lode of citronella candles doesn't seem to be doing the trick and the "bug spray" smells like something the government banned in WWII. You've been assured the insects are harmless but, given their mutant size, it wouldn't hurt to protect yourself as the British colonials did, with a bracing double dose of antimalarial quinine handily available in the form of Pimm's and tonic.

SERVES 1

2 ounces Pimm's No. 1
2 ounces tonic water
splash of grapefruit juice

Pour the Pimm's into a rocks glass filled with ice. Add the tonic water and top with the splash of grapefruit juice.

NUTTY CANDY

YOU'VE RUMMAGED through the kids' bags and inspected every piece of candy for potential allergens. Whew! Another trip to the hospital averted. Luckily, *you* have no allergies—so you've eaten whatever they can't. Now the only nuts in the house are in the liquor cabinet—unless your count yourself, that is.

SERVES 1

1½ ounces amaretto

1½ ounces chocolate liqueur

1½ ounces coconut milk

fun-size chocolate bar, for garnish

Combine the amaretto, chocolate liqueur, and coconut milk in a shaker filled with ice. Shake well (until condensation forms on the entire shaker). Strain into a chilled cocktail glass. Using a vegetable peeler, shave a curl of chocolate on top.

4 HOME-IMPROVEMENT INFUSEMENTS

WHAT'S MORE RELAXING THAN BEING HOME?

Off from work, stretched out on the couch or the recliner, your cares temporarily forgotten . . . unless, of course, you happen to glance at the cobwebs hanging from the ceiling or the peeling wallpaper. Just close your eyes and forget about them . . . until you hear the door hinge that needs to be oiled or the drip that needs to be stopped or the scrabble of that cunning little rodent that needs to be, ah, dispatched to another celestial plane.

Most of the time, you're too busy with your vital charity work/managing your hedge fund/playing Second Life to see the slight imperfections in your home sweet home. After all, it's not like the pet stain on the rug or the broken lock on the bathroom door or the stench emanating from the vegetable crisper are all *that* noticeable. Or, at least, they're not *hurting* anyone.

So none of it is *really* a problem—until your new paramour/playgroup/Junior League president plans a visit to your humble abode. Suddenly, when anticipating the view through their eyes, you see every blemish.

With little time to spare, you run out to the home-improvement store and drop a bundle on the necessary supplies—and it's only when you get started that you realize you don't know your spackle from your grout, you have two brown thumbs, and the last time you applied color to a wall, it was *you* who got the shellacking.

Luckily, it's easy to enhance your home by expertly constructing a round of cocktails. And if you nail that one critical technical skill, your visitors won't notice that anything else is in disrepair.

NAME YOUR POISON

IT TOOK some doing, but you've finally gotten rid of that huge patch of nasty weeds in the backyard. What a sense of accomplishment! Except now you've got an itch on your arms, and on your legs, and on . . . everything else. Mix up a batch of this soothing, calamine-pink, frozen strawberry delight for relief from the inside out.

SERVES 1

1 ounce light rum

1 ounce strawberry liqueur

1½ ounces (3 tablespoons) simple syrup (page 112)

2 ounces milk

¾ cup frozen strawberries (about 10 medium strawberries)

4 ice cubes

fresh strawberry, for garnish

Combine all the ingredients except the fresh strawberry in a blender. Blend until smooth. Pour into a highball glass. Slice the strawberry halfway up from the bottom (don't cut all the way through) and perch it on the rim of the glass. Serve with a straw.

RUSTY NAIL

THE GUY on television made renovation look so easy, but a sharp, protruding object has caught you unawares. As long as you're heading out for a tetanus shot, swing by the liquor store to pick up some classic drink fixings. After a day like this, the nail isn't the only thing that needs to get hammered.

SERVES 1

1½ ounces scotch
1 ounce Drambuie

Fill a chilled rocks glass with ice. Add the scotch to the glass, then the Drambuie.

DO-IT-YOURSELFER'S ESSENTIAL VOCABULARY LESSON

When there are little ears listening, it's helpful to have some substitutes for the words you *really* want to use:

You lose your grip on the nail and it falls onto the floor = DANG!

You accidentally drop the hammer onto the floor = SHOOT!

You hit the nail with the hammer, but it bent = SON OF A GUN!

You hit your thumb with the hammer = F#¢%! (What? You'd rather they learn it on the streets?)

GARDEN PEST CONTROL FROM A TO Z

All-natural, organic insect repellents

Deer-proof fencing

Pesticide

Squirrel-foiling bird feeders

u**Z**i

DIRTY RAVAGED GARDEN-TINI

DESPITE $357 worth of preventative measures, Bambi's relations have decimated your lovingly planted garden—and now you have a hankering for venison. Stem the deer-icidal impulse and use what's left to make this tomato-and-basil-infused beverage. It'll restore your love of all creatures great and small.

SERVES 1

two 1" wedges ripe, juicy tomato (a scant ¼ cup)

3 fresh basil leaves, washed and roughly torn

½ ounce dry vermouth

2 ounces pepper-flavored vodka

1 teaspoon brine from jar of pimiento-stuffed olives

2 pimiento-stuffed olives, for garnish

1 grape tomato, for garnish

In the bottom of a cocktail shaker, using a muddler or a wooden spoon, muddle the wedges of tomato and the basil. Add the vermouth, vodka, and olive brine and fill the shaker with ice. Shake well (until condensation forms on the entire shaker). Strain into a cocktail glass. Skewer the olives and grape tomato alternately on a cocktail pick and place in the glass.

37–1

BITTERSWEET VICTORY

YOU NAGGED and nagged, and your significant other finally agreed to his fair share of the household chores. Too bad he broke three pieces of fine china while loading the dishwasher. Cleanse away the annoyance with this tall Campari cooler. Then order a set of unbreakable plates for him to practice on.

SERVES 1

3 ounces Campari, well chilled

4 to 5 ounces lemon-lime soda, preferably all-natural, well chilled

lime wedge

Pour the Campari into a collins glass with ice. Top with the soda. Squeeze the lime into the glass and drop in the spent lime. Stir gently to mix.

NOTE: For best shelf life, Campari should be refrigerated after opening.

SUPERMARKET CHECKLIST

Sure, it's great to get help with the errands—and grocery shopping is your least favorite. But it's time to take back responsibility if, despite your best training efforts, your spouse repeatedly forgets:

- To bring the coupons with him
- To check the sale circular
- To buy milk
- To buy your personal hygiene products
- To bring the children home with him

DECORATOR'S DREAM

EVERYONE CLAIMS it's so *difficult* to combine florals, plaids, and stripes, but you just have an *eye* for it . . . although you *have* noticed that people tend to tense up a wee bit when they walk in. Obviously, they're not used to *style*—so it might be best to serve them cocktails with a straightforward lemon-on-lemon flavor scheme. And maybe it will help to remove the leopard throw pillows.

SERVES 1

sugar, for rimming

lemon wedge, for rimming

2 ounces Lemon-Infused Vodka (page 115), or store-bought stored in freezer

1½ ounces Downturn Limoncello (page 61) or store-bought version, stored in freezer

½ ounce (1 tablespoon) fresh lemon juice

thin curl of lemon peel, for garnish

Place the sugar into a saucer larger than the diameter of your cocktail glass. Run the lemon wedge around the rim of the glass and dip the rim into the sugar. Chill the glass in the freezer for 10 minutes or more. Combine the vodka, limoncello, and lemon juice in a shaker filled with ice. Shake well (until condensation forms on the entire shaker). Strain into the rimmed, chilled cocktail glass. Hang the lemon peel on the rim.

DEMOLITION DAIQUIRI

THE CONTRACTOR promised that the bathroom expansion would be done in five days, but two months after he broke through the walls, you're still begging your hot showers from a rotation of neighbors . . . and still finding Sheetrock in every crevice. Rinse your mouth with a rum-and-apricot refresher and chalk up the dust to renovation-as-usual.

SERVES 1

sugar, for rimming

lime wedge, for rimming

1½ ounces dark rum

1 ounce apricot liqueur

¾ ounce (1½ tablespoons) fresh lime juice

Place the sugar in a saucer that's slightly larger in diameter than your cocktail glass. Run the lime wedge around the glass to moisten the rim, then dip the glass in the sugar. Chill the glass in the freezer for 10 minutes or more. Place the dark rum, apricot liqueur, and lime juice in a cocktail shaker filled with ice. Shake well (until condensation forms on the entire shaker). Strain the mixture into the chilled, rimmed glass.

SILVER LINING

YOU COME home from a few days away to find you have a swimming pool—in your basement. Who knew such a little leak could cause so much trouble? After you call the plumber and the insurance adjuster, whip yourself up a frozen silver-tequila-and-mango margarita and look on the bright side: Now there's no need to decide what to do with Grandmama's old photo albums.

SERVES 1

coarse salt, for rimming (optional)

lime slice, for rimming (optional)

1½ ounces silver tequila

1 ounce orange liqueur (such as triple sec)

1½ ounces (3 tablespoons) fresh lime juice

2 ounces (4 tablespoons) light agave nectar (see Note) or simple syrup (page 112)

¾ cup frozen mango chunks (see Note)

If a salted rim is desired, pour the salt into a shallow saucer that's a bit wider than the glass. Run the lime wedge around the rim of a margarita glass, then dip it into the salt.

Put the tequila, orange liqueur, lime juice, and agave nectar into a blender. Add the frozen mango chunks and blend until smooth. Pour into the rimmed glass.

NOTE: Frozen mango chunks are available in the frozen-fruit section of your grocer's freezer. If you prefer, peel a ripe mango and cut it into 1-inch chunks; freeze until firm.

Agave nectar is a natural sweetener from the same plant as tequila and is available in most grocery stores, usually near the honey.

MARVEY WALL-HANGER

THE WALLPAPER pattern is *gorgeous,* and it cost a mint—but your vertical stripes are drifting to the right of your plumb line and the self-adhesive is in fact sticking only to itself instead of to the wall. Time to apply the do-it-yourself principle to your refreshments—and as you sip on this "Czeched" twist on a Harvey Wallbanger, consider that maybe a simple coat of paint *is* the way to go.

SERVES 1

1½ ounces vodka

½ ounce Becherovka liqueur

⅔ cup (6 ounces) orange juice

Combine the vodka, Becherovka, and orange juice in a shaker filled with ice. Shake well (until condensation forms on the entire shaker). Strain the mixture into a collins glass filled with ice.

TOOLBOX STAND-INS

Guys, why go through all the trouble of digging out your toolbox when there are substitutes so close at hand?

IF YOU NEED:	TRY:
a hammer	the heel of a shoe
WD-40	baby oil
a screwdriver	a butter knife
a wood file	a PedEgg®

YOUR WEEKNIGHTS AND WEEKENDS ARE FILLED with a long checklist of errands and appointments: You have to get the dog to his vet/groomer/behavioral specialist! You have to get the kids to soccer/religious instruction/the psychopharmacologist! You have get the food shopping done before staying home for the Saturday furniture-delivery window of 8 a.m. to 7 p.m., but unless you pick up your dry cleaning at some point between 9 and 5, you'll have nothing to wear to work on Monday.

Errands, errands, errands. Despite the increased convenience of the Internet for shopping/driver's-license renewal/parole check-in, there seems to be no escape from last-minute supermarket runs for the forgotten pound of butter, from the inconvenient appliance breakdown, from that unplanned meeting with the guidance counselor.

It wouldn't be so bad if you could rely on chores to go like clock-work—if you could count on getting a parking space right away, or getting the correct washing machine part you ordered the first time. Life would be easier if you could see your doctor at the 2 p.m. appointment time instead of sitting in the waiting room until 3:42. Or if you could count on the line at the grocery store to move quickly—instead of stalling interminably because your cashier is "in training" or the computer just went down or the person just ahead of you is having a pricing dispute/writing an out-of-state check/paying with pennies.

But it seems more often than not, daily life is full of unexpected nuisances that stall your forward motion. So when your day hasn't gone as expected and your list of "To Dos" remains woefully undone, go home, make yourself a cocktail, and revel in the fact that at least in mixing a delicious drink you accomplished something useful.

CLEANING FLUID

THE BIG presentation is at the crack of dawn Monday, and it seems your best suit has shrunk! That's the third time this has happened—you're just going to have to switch dry cleaners. While you survey your wardrobe for something that hasn't been ruined, make yourself a dry, grappa cocktail. That's funny, the shirt is tight, too—and you washed it yourself . . .

SERVES 1

2 ounces grappa

1 ounce sweet vermouth

splash of maraschino-cherry juice

3 dashes Angostura bitters

maraschino cherry, for garnish

Add all the ingredients to a cocktail shaker filled with ice. Shake well (until condensation forms on the entire shaker). Strain into a chilled cocktail glass. Add the maraschino cherry.

127-2

UNDER THE HOOD

Car giving you trouble? Don't twiddle your thumbs like a novice—try these tactics to impress your passengers:

- Open the hood, peer solemnly at the motor and say, "GEEZ! Who %$#@! the %$#@! valve, %$#@!'s sake?"

- Take your T-shirt off and use it to wipe the dipstick (guys, this works best if you have tattoos and know where/what the dipstick is; ladies, this is highly effective in attracting more qualified help).

- If you don't see the motor (the big thing in the middle) or the dipstick (you're on your own there), you're probably looking in the trunk. Quickly save face by saying: "GEEZ! Who %$#@! took the %$#@! jumper cables out?"

- Make sure to have AAA on speed dial.

EN-GIN TROUBLE

USED TO be you could take apart a muscle car and put it together with your eyes closed. But since computer chips seem to be replacing all the moving parts, now you practically need a degree from M.I.T. to put in a new spark plug. Since you won't be driving anytime soon, fill *your* tank with a high-test mixture of gin and V8, with added horsepower and a pepper kick. It's strong enough to clean a carburetor.

SERVES 1

1½ ounces gin

½ ounce (1 tablespoon) fresh lime juice

4 ounces (½ cup) V8 vegetable juice

1 tablespoon prepared horseradish, or to taste

½ teaspoon Worcestershire sauce

3 dashes Tabasco sauce, or to taste

freshly ground black pepper

lime "wheel," for garnish

Combine the gin, lime juice, V8, horseradish, Worcestershire sauce, and Tabasco sauce in a shaker filled with ice. Roll the shaker gently to mix, then strain the mixture into a rocks glass filled with ice. Grind pepper on top and hang the lime slice on the rim of the glass.

HOLDING PATTERN

YOU'VE TRIED every option on the automated "help" line, but the electronic voice on the other end has begun to adopt a condescending tone. While you experience your "longer than average" wait to speak to a warm body, put the Muzak on speaker and mix up a batch of crisp raspberry-and-white-wine cocktails. Help yourself to one—or a few—and you'll be waiting for service, with a smile.

SERVES 6

- 1 pint (2 cups) fresh raspberries
- 6 ounces (¾ cup) simple syrup (page 112)
- one 750 ml. bottle dry white wine (such as sauvignon blanc), well chilled
- 12 ounces (1½ cups) club soda, well chilled

Reserve 18 raspberries for garnish. Using a muddler or a wooden spoon, in a small bowl, muddle remaining raspberries with the simple syrup. Allow to steep for at least 15 minutes, up to 2 hours (you can steep the mixture longer, but if you do, refrigerate it). When ready to serve, divide the mixture among six tall glasses ¾ full of ice. Pour approximately 4 ounces of wine into each glass. Top each glass with about 2 ounces of club soda and stir gently. Drop 3 raspberries into each glass.

It's a good instrument to use because back of it there are friendly and competent people serving you . . . about 300,000 of them

BELL TELEPHONE SYSTEM

PROPANE PROXY

YOU'VE INVITED a dozen people—including your boss—for a barbecue and you've got a king's ransom worth of meat on the grill . . . only to discover you're out of propane and the gas station is closed for the night. Fill your guests' tanks with a delicious sake cocktail—after two rounds, nobody will notice the menu has changed to steak tartare.

SERVES 1

4 ounces (½ cup) sake

½ ounce (1 tablespoon) Ginger-Lime-Infused Simple Syrup (page 112)

2 ounces blood-orange juice

Pour the sake, simple syrup, and blood-orange juice into a shaker filled with ice. Shake well (until condensation forms on the entire shaker). Strain into a chilled cocktail glass.

THE LION IN WINTER

Ladies: Is your husband King of the Grill but shy of the stove? Follow these simple suggestions for "winterizing" the barbecue process, and your man will be taking over dinner duty, all year round!

- Install an outdoor heat lamp
- Buy him ski gloves—no need for barbecue mitts!
- Set up an area for the portable flat-screen television
- Move his masssaging recliner to within arm's length of the grill
- Tap a keg next to the propane tank

FIREMAN'S SOUR

IT'S THE third time the alarm has gone off this week and the neighbors are beginning to refer to your house as "the one with the fire engines in front." Apologize again for wasting the firefighters' time and, when the smoke clears, make yourself their namesake rum sour. You might even consider their suggestion that you clean your oven.

SERVES 1

2 ounces light rum

1 ounce
(2 tablespoons)
fresh lime juice

½ ounce (1 tablespoon)
Cranadine Syrup
(page 114)

lime slice, for garnish

maraschino cherry,
for garnish

Combine the rum, lime juice, and Cranadine Syrup in a cocktail shaker filled with ice. Shake well (until condensation forms on the entire shaker). Strain into a rocks glass filled with ice. Skewer the lime slice and maraschino cherry on a decorative pick and add to the glass.

STICKER-SHOCK SANGRIA

THE PRICES of milk and bread seem to go up every week. And you'd love to buy all-organic but, given the cost of the meat, you suspect they've been feeding the animals gold bullion instead of grass. Luckily, you can make a potluck sangria from practically whatever fruit is on sale, any flavor brandy you have on hand, and your favorite "two-buck" wine.

SERVES 8–10

1 cup each of two types ripe fruit, chopped into ½" pieces (see Note)

8 ounces (1 cup) fruit brandy or liqueur (see Note)

One 750 ml. bottle inexpensive red or white wine, well chilled

1 liter club soda, well chilled

In a pitcher, combine the fruit and the brandy or liqueur and allow to macerate for at least 2 hours, preferably overnight in the refrigerator. When ready to serve, add the chilled wine and club soda to the pitcher. Stir. Serve a bit of the fruit in each glass.

NOTE: You can play with different combinations of fruits and liqueurs—in general, stone fruits and berries are nice with lighter liqueurs and white wine; apples and pears are great with heavier liqueurs and red wine; oranges go with either.

RECYCLED CUP

THE NUMBER in the little triangle is blurry—and you're getting eye strain trying to figure out if it reads a recyclable "2" or a ditchable "5." And how clean does that aluminum lasagna pan have to be before you can put it in the bin—or are you expending more fossil fuel with the hot water it would take to wash it? Your garbage is no longer clogging landfills—but now it's draining your brain. As you rip the plastic window from your box of facial tissues, reduce the impact with an apple-orange treat—out of a reusable glass, please.

SERVES 1

1 ounce apple brandy

½ ounce triple sec

3 dashes orange bitters (such as Fee's)

4 ounces (½ cup) hard (alcoholic) cider, well chilled

2 ounces club soda, well chilled

orange slice, for garnish

Combine the apple brandy, triple sec, and bitters in a shaker filled with ice. Shake well (until condensation forms on the entire shaker). Strain the mixture into a highball glass full of ice. Add the cider and club soda and stir gently. Perch the orange slice on the side of the glass.

DIG IN
and
DIG OUT the SCRAP
Save
METALS
RAGS
PAPER
BONES
RUBBER
GLASS
THEY ARE VITAL WAR NEEDS
GET IN TOUCH WITH YOUR LOCAL COMMITTEE
ISSUED BY PUBLIC INFORMATION, FOR NATIONAL SALVAGE OFFICE, OTTAWA;

6 VACATION LIBATIONS

THE PAST FEW MONTHS IN THE OFFICE HAVE BEEN pure torture, and the only thing that's gotten you through is the thought of your long-awaited, carefully planned vacation. It's the chance to leave behind the workaday grind and escape to the warm embrace of a tropical paradise/European café society/your fellow Trekkies. It's the respite from the day-to-day cares and irritations and complete immersion in . . . a whole new and different set of cares and irritations.

When you paid for the week in the getaway cabin, you were dreaming of floating on an inner tube in an ol' swimming hole . . . but you didn't imagine you'd have to walk a quarter mile to the bathroom, through swarms of mosquitoes the size of Texas. When you booked your trip abroad, you envisioned being captivated by the art at some of the world's great museums . . . but instead you're held captive by fluctuating currencies, lunatic cabbies who drive 100 miles an hour on the wrong side of the road, and your inability to remember the difference between "Men's Room" and "Ladies' Room" in French/Arabic/Swahili. When you carefully saved for that once-in-a-lifetime locale, you were thinking of sybaritic relaxation in exotic surroundings—until you arrive to find out the water's undrinkable, it's shark season, and the U.S.-installed puppet government has just been overthrown by the local warlords.

Yes, vacations can be overbooked with worries—but a getaway that's gotten away from you is no reason to derail. From absinthe to Zima, some form of alcoholic beverage is available *nearly* worldwide. And with the right "vacation in a glass," your travel troubles are up, up, and away!

BLACKBERRY CURSE

VACATION USED to mean you didn't have to think about the office. Now everyone expects you to respond to e-mail. You purposely picked the most remote locale you could think of, but when you pleaded "incommunicado," your boss's assistant plotted the location of every cell tower on your itinerary. Of course, you do have *another* hand-held solution—so when your pocket vibrates, reach for the contraband blackberry beverage in your handy flask . . .

SERVES 1

4 or 5 fresh (or frozen, thawed) blackberries, plus extra for ice cubes (optional)

1½ ounces blackberry schnapps

½ ounce (1 tablespoon) Thyme-Infused Simple Syrup (page 113)

½ ounce (1 tablespoon) fresh lime juice

Berry Pretty Ice Cubes (page 116, optional)

2 to 3 ounces club soda, well chilled

thyme sprig, for garnish

Muddle the blackberries in a shaker with the blackberry schnapps. Add the simple syrup and lime juice and fill the shaker with plain ice. Shake well (until condensation forms on the entire shaker). Strain into a collins glass, over two blackberry ice cubes (if using). Add the club soda and stir gently. Add the thyme sprig to the glass.

TOUR DE GLASS

YOU THOUGHT you looked race-ready in your *très chic* new shorts, but the English-speaking guy at Mon Chéri's Bicycle Rental suggested you take advantage of their E-Z Ryder "American Around Town" model—the one with the extra-roomy shopping basket and the Comfort Width seat. Shift gears, head back to the *maison d'été* for a little Lillet-based "sports drink"—and bottoms up!

SERVES 1

3 fresh peach slices, plus one slice for garnish

1½ ounces light rum

4 ounces (½ cup) Lillet Blanc, well chilled

With a muddler or a wooden spoon, muddle the 3 peach slices and rum in the bottom of a highball glass. Fill the glass with ice and add the Lillet. Drop the remaining peach slice into the glass.

BE PREPARED

Active vacations present their own set of challenges. Woe to the enthusiast who forgets to bring along the appropriate safety gear and essentials for his or her chosen sport.

BIKERS
- padded shorts
- first–aid kit
- water bottle

CANOERS
- waterproof shoes
- life jacket
- canteen

HIKERS
- sturdy boots
- emergency whistle
- hip flask

SKIERS
- goggles
- hand- and feet-warmers
- St. Bernard

MOTHER'S MAI TAI

DISHWASHER, washing machine, clothes dryer: Your husband said your vacation condo would have "all the comforts of home" like it was a *good* thing. Next year, you'll go *without* him and the kids and rent a cabana boy to serve you tropical cocktails.

SERVES 1

1 ounce light rum

1 ounce dark rum

1 ounce triple sec

½ ounce (1 tablespoon) Cranadine Syrup (page 114)

½ ounce (1 tablespoon) orgeat (almond) syrup or ½ ounce amaretto

½ ounce (1 tablespoon) fresh lime juice

pineapple chunk, for garnish

maraschino cherry, for garnish

Pour the light rum, dark rum, triple sec, Cranadine Syrup, orgeat syrup, and lime juice into a shaker filled with ice. Shake well (until condensation forms on the entire shaker). Strain the mixture into a double old-fashioned glass. Spear the pineapple chunk and maraschino cherry onto a decorative pick and add it to the glass.

NAKED INHIBITION

WHEN YOU put down the nonrefundable deposit, you thought "Nakation" was a Native American term, but the trip organizer has informed you of the unadorned truth. Don't relegate yourself to the "prude" beach: Screw up your courage with a cucumber-infused treat . . . garnish optional.

SERVES 1

2-inch length of salad cucumber (see Note), peeled and chopped into ¼-inch chunks, plus one ¼-inch unpeeled slice for garnish

6 large, fresh mint leaves, washed and torn in half, plus sprig for garnish

1 ounce dry vermouth

2 ounces gin

With a muddler or a wooden spoon, muddle the cucumber and mint together with the vermouth in the bottom of a cocktail shaker. Fill the shaker with ice. Add the gin and shake well (until condensation forms on the entire shaker). Strain into a cocktail glass. Hang the cucumber slice on the edge of the glass and put the mint sprig in the glass.

NOTE: For best results, use a seeded salad variety of cucumber. The English variety (often called "seedless" or "burpless" and typically wrapped in plastic) yields less juice—and therefore, less flavor—when muddled.

ASTORIA ICED TEA

THE TRAFFIC was so bad you could've gone to *Greece* in the time it took to drive to "a quick, relaxing weekend at the beach"—and you think the "shortcut" added about an hour. When you finally arrive, commemorate your journey's end with something cool, refreshing—and potent.

SERVES 1

½ ounce gin

½ ounce ouzo

½ ounce rum

½ ounce triple sec

½ ounce vodka

½ ounce (1 tablespoon) fresh lemon juice

½ ounce (1 tablespoon) simple syrup (page 112)

4 ounces (½ cup) cola, well chilled

lemon wedge, for garnish

licorice stick, for garnish

Pour the gin, ouzo, rum, triple sec, vodka, lemon juice, and simple syrup into a shaker filled with ice. Shake well (until condensation forms on the entire shaker). Strain the mixture into a highball glass filled with ice. Top with the cola and stir gently. Add the lemon wedge and licorice stick to the glass.

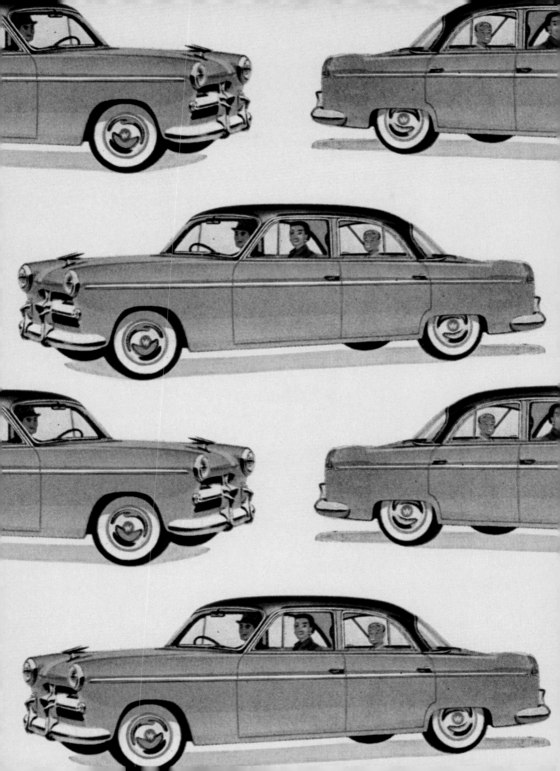

CUB REPORTERS

Kids—here's a neat way to have fun and earn some extra spending money during vacation: Play "Paparazzi"! Use Dad's telephoto lens to take pictures of the neighbors sunbathing. Create a supermarket-tabloid-like "cellulite" article on the family computer. Print and sell for $1 a copy.

Better yet, save the environment with the "less paper" option: Show a "mock-up" of the article to the featured neighbors and ask for $20 from each to *not* print and sell it!

LARGE-QUANTITY AND ALL-AGES LEMON-LIME AID SERVES 16

For all-ages gatherings, omit the gin from the recipe and serve it on the side, to allow people to mix their own.

1 cup (8 ounces) simple syrup (page 112), well chilled

1 cup (8 ounces) lemon juice, well chilled

1 cup (8 ounces) lime juice, well chilled

One 750 ml. bottle gin

2 liters club soda, well chilled

iceberg (page 117)

Combine the simple syrup, lemon juice, lime juice, and gin in a large beverage cooler. Add the iceberg, then the club soda. Stir to mix.

STAND-OUT LEMON-LIME AID

WHEN YOUR innkeeper told you about the scenic stroll, she didn't mention it was four miles, straight uphill. Of course, on the way, a couple of local urchins are selling refreshments at usurious prices. If only the little hooligans were old enough to sell gin at their "ade" stand . . . then it would all be downhill from there.

SERVES 1

1½ ounces gin

½ ounce (1 tablespoon) simple syrup (page 112)

½ ounce (1 tablespoon) fresh lemon juice

½ ounce (1 tablespoon) fresh lime juice

4 ounces (½ cup) club soda, well chilled

curl of lemon peel, for garnish

Pour the gin, simple syrup, lemon juice, and lime juice into a cocktail shaker filled with ice. Shake well (until condensation forms on the entire shaker). Strain the mixture into a collins glass filled with ice. Fill the glass with the club soda; stir to mix. Add the lemon peel to the glass.

SEÑOR STAYCATION
(aka "The Michelada")

BOWLING ALLEY, scenic overlook, mall—who needs to deal with the problems of long-distance travel when you've got so many cultural adventures right in your own hometown? In fact, who needs to go anywhere? Just add a spicy Mexican kick to your usual beer and ride the lawn chair to destination relaxation!

SERVES 1

1 lime, washed and cut in half

coarse salt, for rimming

¼ teaspoon Maggi Seasoning Sauce (see Note) or substitute 3 dashes of soy sauce (preferably naturally brewed) plus ¼ teaspoon Worcestershire sauce

3 dashes hot sauce (such as Tabasco), or to taste

12-ounce bottle of beer, preferably Mexican, frosty cold

freshly ground black pepper

Run half of the lime around a pilsner glass. Place salt in a shallow saucer slightly wider in diameter than the rim of the glass. Dip the dampened glass rim in the salt to coat. Chill the glass for 10 minutes or more. Squeeze the juice of both halves of the lime into the glass. Add the Maggi seasoning and hot sauce and mix. Add the beer. Garnish with a grind of black pepper.

NOTE: Maggi Seasoning Sauce is a dark liquid in a bottle with a bright yellow label and cap. It is available at many grocers, especially those who carry a selection of Hispanic specialties. To order online, see Resources (page 120).

AUG • 60

THE ONE-PIECE (NONALCOHOLIC) SERVES 1

1½ ounces Cranadine Syrup (page 114)

6 ounces grapefruit juice, well chilled

2 ounces club soda, well chilled

Combine the Cranadine Syrup and grapefruit juice in a tall glass ¾ filled with ice. Add the club soda. Stir to mix.

THE SANDY BATHING SUIT

YOU CAN'T remember how you got talked into it, but it may have had something to do with that liquid grapefruit-and-pomegranate bribe. Now that you're up to your neck in sand—and there's sand up in every other body part—you'd think they'd at least give you a straw so you could finish the drink.

SERVES 1

1½ ounces grapefruit-
flavored vodka

1 ounce pomegranate
liqueur

4 ounces (½ cup) pure
grapefruit juice,
well chilled

straw, for serving

Pour the vodka and pomegranate liqueur into a tall glass ¾ filled with ice. Add the grapefruit juice and stir. Serve with a straw.

SUSPICIOUS PACKAGE

WELL, YOU couldn't drag four pieces of luggage with you into the john, now, could you? And the guy who offered to watch your stuff seemed so nice—said he was in the spice trade. At least the dogs have stopped following you, and the security guard offered you some refreshments while you're being detained. What would taste good right now is something fruity and a little exotic. Maybe pear—and cardamom's big here in Turkey, isn't it?

SERVES 1

1 ounce Cardamom-Infused Simple Syrup (page 113)

2 ounces pear brandy

3 dashes of orange bitters (such as Fee's)

¼" x ¼" x 3" "stick" of fresh pear, for garnish

lemon juice, to prevent the pear garnish from browning

Combine the simple syrup, pear brandy, and orange bitters in a cocktail shaker filled with ice. Shake well (until condensation forms on the entire shaker). Strain into a chilled cocktail glass. Brush the pear stick with the lemon juice to prevent browning, and add to the glass.

TRAVELER'S ADVISORY

There are some places in the world where beliefs prohibit drinking alcoholic beverages. *Peterson's* advises using *extreme caution* when booking trips to Muslim nations, the state of Utah, or yoga retreats, where availability might be limited.

BASIC RECIPES AND TECHNIQUES

Do try these at home—they're all easy to make and, in the case of the syrups and the vodka, they'll last quite a while in the refrigerator or freezer, so you can make them well in advance of parties.

SYRUPS AND PUREES

SIMPLEST SIMPLE SYRUP

When the recipe calls for "simple syrup," use this recipe.

MAKES APPROXIMATELY 1½ CUPS

1 cup sugar
1 cup water

Combine the sugar and water in a small saucepan over medium heat. Bring to a simmer, stirring occasionally until all the sugar dissolves and the mixture is clear. Cool. Store in an airtight glass jar for up to 1 month in the refrigerator.

INFUSED SIMPLE SYRUPS

Stir up an ounce or two with club soda and ice for an all-natural soft drink.

Ginger-Lime-Infused Simple Syrup

MAKES APPROXIMATELY 1½ CUPS

1 cup sugar
1 cup water
3-inch piece fresh ginger, peeled and cut into 6 chunks
zest of 2 limes

Combine the sugar, water, ginger, and lime zest in a small saucepan over medium heat. Bring to a simmer, stirring occasionally until the sugar dissolves and the mixture is clear. Turn off the heat and allow the ginger and lime to steep in the syrup for 3 hours. Strain the syrup into an airtight glass jar. Store for up to 1 month in the refrigerator.

THYME-INFUSED SIMPLE SYRUP

Substitute 12 sprigs of fresh thyme for the ginger and lime.

CARDAMOM-INFUSED SIMPLE SYRUP

Substitute 12 pods of green cardamom, lightly crushed, for the ginger and lime.

DATE-ORANGE PUREE

MAKES APPROXIMATELY 1¼ CUPS

2½ cups water
¼ cup sugar
1 cup pitted dates, packed
1 tablespoon orange zest

Combine all the ingredients and bring to a boil in a small saucepan. Reduce the heat and simmer until the dates are completely mushy and disintegrating and the liquid is reduced to a level where it just covers the dates. Allow to cool. Pour into a blender and liquefy. Store in an airtight jar in the refrigerator. You can make this puree up to 3 days in advance. Stir before using.

NOTE: The leftover puree tastes good on pancakes!

CRANADINE SYRUP
(AKA POMEGRANATE-CRANBERRY SYRUP)

Store-bought grenadine often includes things not found in nature. This homemade version is easy; the addition of cranberry to the traditional pomegranate brightens the intense flavor and the color. You can substitute purchased grenadine, if you need to.

MAKES ABOUT 1¾ CUPS

1 cup (8 ounces) pure cranberry juice

1 cup (8 ounces) pure pomegranate juice

1½ cups sugar

Combine the cranberry juice, pomegranate juice, and sugar in a small saucepan. Over medium heat, bring the mixture to a boil. Reduce the heat and keep the mixture at a low boil until it has thickened slightly and reduced to about 1¾ cups, about 25 to 30 minutes. Store in an airtight jar and refrigerate for up to 1 month. The mixture will thicken a bit more with refrigeration.

INFUSED LIQUORS
GINGER-LEMONGRASS-INFUSED VODKA

2 stalks fresh lemongrass, ends cut and trimmed of dry leaves

6-inch piece fresh ginger, peeled and cut into ½-inch-thick rounds

6 cups (48 ounces) vodka

SPECIAL EQUIPMENT: 6-cup glass jar with airtight lid

Slice the lemongrass in half lengthwise, then into thirds (you should wind up with pieces of stalk 4" to 5" long). Place the ginger and lemongrass in the jar, then pour in the vodka. Close the lid and let the mixture steep for at least 2 weeks in a cool, dry place, shaking occasionally to mix. After 2 weeks, taste the vodka every day or so until you're happy with the strength of the infusion. At that point, decant the contents into clean, airtight bottles, straining out the ginger, lemongrass, and any sediment from them. Store in a cool, dry place or, better yet, in your freezer, where it will keep indefinitely.

LEMON-INFUSED VODKA
MAKES 1 LITER

8 lemons, well scrubbed

1 liter vodka

SPECIAL EQUIPMENT:
2-quart glass jar with airtight lid

With a sharp vegetable peeler or paring knife, peel the lemons in continuous spirals about ½-inch wide. With the knife, scrape all white pith from the inside of the lemon peel. Place in a 2-quart glass jar and pour the vodka over it, making sure the lemon peels are completely immersed in the vodka. Allow to steep in a cool place away from direct sunlight, shaking occasionally. After one week, begin to taste every day or so. When the vodka has the desired infusion of lemon flavor, strain the mixture into a bottle (for Downturn Limoncello recipe, page 61, steep for at least 2 weeks before using). Store in a cool, dry place or, preferably, in your freezer.

ICE, ICE BABY

Ice is an important component in your Happy Hour concoctions. When making your own, it's best to use filtered water so the cubes don't impart any off flavors. If you don't have an ice crusher to crush ice: Place it in a zip-top freezer bag, put the bag on a chopping board (and a stable surface), and whale away on it with a hammer. If the bag rips, place it inside another freezer bag and continue hammering.

DECORATIVE ICE CUBES
Decorative ice cubes add visual appeal to a cocktail or mocktail. Make them ahead of time and store them, by type, in zip-top bags in the freezer until ready to use.

BERRY PRETTY ICE CUBES

Wash berries and place them in individual compartments of an ice-cube tray. Fill the tray with water to just barely cover fruit and freeze.

A-PEELING ICE CUBES

Using a zester, cut thin, curly peels of citrus and place one curl in each individual compartment of an ice-cube tray. Fill the tray with water to cover the peels and freeze.

COOL AS . . . CUBES

Slice an unpeeled cucumber lengthwise into quarters; slice each quarter into ¼-inch wedges. Put a wedge of cucumber in each individual compartment of an ice-cube tray. Fill the tray with water to cover the cucumber and freeze.

HERBACEOUS ICE CUBES

Use mint, thyme, basil—depending on the recipe in which you're using them. Wash the herbs well. Put a sprig of the desired herb in each individual compartment of an ice-cube tray. Fill the tray with water to cover each sprig and freeze.

HALF-JUICE ICE CUBES

Making ice cubes with half juice can minimize the dilution of a drink that contains juice, such as a punch, mocktail, or ade. (Water freezes more firmly, so these will melt more slowly than all-juice cubes, though more quickly than all-water cubes.) To make them, pour a mixture of one part water to one part of the desired juice into ice-cube trays and freeze.

ICEBERGS

Large pieces of ice melt more slowly and are best for keeping large quantities of drinks—like punches and ades—cool.

Icebergs are large, square cubes made from the bottom of well-washed wax-paper milk or juice cartons. Cut off the tops of the cartons; you want the end result to be a perfect cube. Icebergs take a while to freeze solid, so be sure to start them a day before you need them. Freezing in two layers will ensure there's decorative fruit throughout. For an average-sized punch bowl, use 3 or 4 quart-sized 'bergs (2¾ inches square) or 1 or 2 half-gallon-sized 'berg (3¾ inches square).

PEACHY TEA ICEBERGS

These are good for the Fish-Story Punch (page 58). The first amount given is for the quart-sized cartons; amounts for the larger 'bergs are in parentheses.

For each 'berg, pour ⅔ cup (1½ cups) brewed, cooled black tea (i.e., the same tea that's in the punch) into the desired carton. Cut up a ripe peach and put a few slices in each carton. Allow to freeze until set, about 2 to 3 hours. Repeat this sequence to create another layer of tea and fruit in each of the cartons (this ensures there will be fruit throughout the 'berg). Allow time to freeze completely, preferably overnight.

ICE RINGS

Any of the decorative ideas for ice cubes can be used in an ice ring, or make one with juice (such as pear juice for the Hole Punch, page 42) or a mixture of juice and water. At least a day before it's needed, fill a ring mold (see Resources, page 120) or Bundt pan halfway with water. Place well-washed fruit or herb "decorations" in the water and freeze until firm (fruit tends to float; freezing in two layers ensures that it will stay in the center). Fill the rest of the mold with water and freeze again until the entire mold is frozen solid.

EQUIPMENT

These cocktail-specific items are useful to have when creating the happy-making concoctions described herein.

BAR SPOON OR ICED-TEA SPOON: for stirring tall drinks

BAR STRAINER: used for straining the liquid from a shaker

CHANNEL KNIFE: a tool for making garnishes. As you run it around a citrus fruit, the channel on the blade digs into the peel to make thin strips.

COCKTAIL PICKS: for skewering garnishes

COCKTAIL SHAKER: for properly mixing and chilling cocktail ingredients. A Boston shaker consists of a clear, tapered bar glass and a metal shaker bottom. When the glass is put into the metal, it creates a seal. After shaking, the seal needs to be broken with a hard hit, usually with the heel of your hand. Metal cocktail shakers come in all shapes and sizes, with a strainer usually built into the top.

CORKSCREW OR OTHER WINE OPENER: for the obvious

JIGGER: for measuring 1 to 2 ounces of liquid, especially liquor

ICE CRUSHER: Some blenders do the job; and there are contraptions designed expressly for the purpose. If you have neither, use the freezer-bag-and-hammer method (page 115).

MEASURING CUPS AND SPOONS: for measuring amounts other than 1 to 2 ounces

MUDDLER OR WOODEN SPOON: for smashing fruits to squish the juice and flavor out of them

SAUCER: or small plate in which to dip the rims of glasses in order to coat them with salt, sugar, etc.

VEGETABLE PEELER: for peeling fruits and making garnishes

GLASSWARE

Here are general descriptions of the most common types called for in the recipes. If you don't have the suggested glass, use something approximate. Or slug it straight from the shaker—who'll know? For "shaker made" cold drinks, it's nice to chill the glassware first if you've got room in your freezer—just stick them in for at least ten minutes, until you're ready to serve.

CHAMPAGNE FLUTE: Tall and thin to preserve the bubbles, it's good for any drink with a little sparkle to it. (Note: Wide champagne coupes have come back into style too.)

COCKTAIL GLASS/MARTINI GLASS: the one with the universal, upside-down-triangle shape that means "A Good Time." Older versions tend to be smaller (4 ounces), while the more recent have been supersized (up to 12 ounces).

COLLINS GLASS: generally tall and straight-sided, holding about 10 to 12 ounces. Daintier than a highball glass and good for when you want to show off the ice.

GELATIN-SHOT CUP: 2 ounces, made of paper or plastic, because they need to be bendable to squoosh out the gelatin. See Resources, page 120.

HIGHBALL GLASS: versatile and slightly wider than a collins glass, holding up to 14 ounces. Arguably the most often used.

MARGARITA GLASS: widemouthed, stemmed, birdbath-like glass. If you don't have them, use a rocks glass.

ROCKS GLASS/OLD-FASHIONED GLASS: short and squat, it's good for drinks that are . . . ah, on the rocks.

PUNCH CUP: has a handle; usually comes in a set with the punch bowl

SHOT GLASS: for measuring, and for . . . shots

WINEGLASS: Generally, a red-wine glass has a wider bowl than a white-wine glass. Some glasses are even manufactured for use with specific varietals but all-purpose wineglasses are fine. They should hold about 12 to 16 ounces (you don't put that much in, of course . . . well, hardly ever).

RESOURCES

LIQUORS

The alcoholic-beverage world is so vast, it's a wonder that there are any "sad hours" at all—or that anyone gets anything done. But it is also a world that is strictly regulated, with buying and shipping laws that vary greatly from state to state. While the varieties and brands of liquor used in the drinks in this book are generally well known and/or widely available, when you're looking for more information or a source for one that's unfamiliar to you, know that your Internet search engine is your friend.

BarSuppliesDirect.com and Kegworks.com
Sources for bar equipment, gelatin-shot cups, etc.

BevMo.com
A great resource for rimming sugars and salts, as well as Torani orgeat syrup and some bitters.

CrateAndBarrel.com, PotteryBarn.com, SurLaTable.com, Williams-Sonoma.com
These are all great resources for glasses and barware.

eBottles.com
Has a huge selection of bottles in all shapes and sizes, for when you want to give away your infused creations.

EZ-Squeeze.com
A site for small cups made specifically for gelatin shots.

FeeBrothers.com
Offers a selection of bitters.

Infused-Vodka.com
Features a selection of fancy bottles for when you want to show off your infusing skills.

MexGrocer.com
A source for Maggi Seasoning Sauce.

Tupperware.com
For the Jel-Ring mold that's good for ice rings.

ACKNOWLEDGMENTS

A thousand thanks to Lauren Shakely and Doris Cooper for their continued faith in Peterson's, and to my editor, Aliza Fogelson, for taking up the Happy Hour reins. Throughout the process I was grateful for the ever-efficient and always-cheerful (even without a cocktail) Peggy Paul.

I was honored to once again be in the hands of the art and production pros at Clarkson Potter—thanks especially to Stephanie Huntwork for her timeless and timely design and for going above and beyond for the cause. My continued gratitude goes to the most excellent Random House sales teams, and to Kate Tyler and Donna Passannante, for their efforts past and present.

I am indebted to photographer Paul D'Innocenzo for his thoughtfulness and flexibility as well as his talent. Vintage purveyor Pam Yosh again generously allowed me to borrow from her wonderful wares—I can't thank her enough. Beverly Peterson's retouching skills beautified time-damaged photos; if only she could do that for me!

Love of photography and archival skills are in Mary Beth Thomas's DNA, and I owe her big for letting me access her vast collections, use her equipment, and exploit her family (pp. 12, 15, 20, 27, 56, 92, 108). For generously exploiting their families and friends, I thank: Theresa Canzoneri (pp. 24, 39), Gregory Citarella (p. 82), Elizabeth Philosophos Cooper (p. 28), Maureen and Jay Daly (pp. 16, 32, 107), Mary Dunn (p. 78), Harry and Edith Firstenberg (p. 5), Janice Fryer and Mildred Fryer (p. 71), Susan Galea (p. 54), Lorraine McSpedon (pp. 60, 96), Erica Okone (pp. 19, 95), Eileen O'Neill (p. 81), Anne and Eddie Parsells (pp. 43, 59), Gail Spagnoli Peterson (pp. 23, 73), Louisa Pricoli (p. 30), Robert and Rowena Peterson (p. 111), Judy San Gregorio (pp. 44, 68), Karin Sedgwick (p. 6), Diane and George Smith (pp. 64, 74), Kerry Jones Stitch (p. 46), and Suzanne Taylor (p. 11).

There would be no Peterson's without my agent, Jen Griffin, and I would have no happy hours without the following people who've helped in many ways, from recipe testing to contact-making to long-distance photo procuring to offering advice and information and unfailing support: Rose

Arlia, Sharron Bauer, the women of the Block Island Cocktail Testing Institute, Lydia Bologna, Maria Bologna, Lynn Citarella and Bill Barthel, Linda Dickey, the Finns and their guinea-pig party guests, Sharon Gamboa, Liz Harwell and Scott Dare, Mary Hoar, Ingrid Kasper, Andrea Kochman, David Latt, Emily Loose, Elizabeth Lyngholm, Ed McSpedon, Amy Nover, Gail O'Rourke, Marge Ginsburg Paone, Eddie and Janie Peterson, Eric Peterson, Laura Peterson, Lisa Peterson, John and Judy Peterson, Stanley and Janet Peterson—heck, in fact all the Petersons and their families! There are too many to list! Lori Poggiagalle, Carolyn Rostkowski, Deborah and Richard Shea, Joan Solano, Richard and Carolyn Tedeschi, the Towers, Joanne Tuccillo, Diane Weingarten, Barbara Yosh, and Pam Yosh.

And, of course, I extend my heartfelt appreciation to the folks who populate these pages; I hope I do justice to their happy hours: Lee and Mal Armstrong (p. 6); Hilda and Otto Buckholtz (p. 6); Charlie the parakeet Canzoneri (p. 24); Salvatore Canzoneri (pp. 24, 39); Charlie Carroll (p. 16); Inga Britt Caruso (p. 111); Bill Charron (pp. 16, 107); Helen Charron (p. 107); Gregory Citarella (p. 82); John and Grace Corradini (p. 30); John Daly (p. 32); Moe Daly (p. 32); Edith and Harry Firstenberg (p. 5); Gordon and Mildred Fryer (p 71); Joseph Galea (p. 54); Joan Gargiulo (p. 96); Dorothy Goodman nee Rodgers (p. 28); Cathy Herde (p. 92); Margaret and Joseph Idiaquez (p. 11); J. Michael Jones, Michael J. Jones and Timothy J. Jones (all p. 46); Doug Keil (p. 59); Russ Lydon (p. 39); Mary Jane McCormick (p. 20); Esther McSpedon (p. 60); Eileen and Mary Mullaly (p. 78); Ed and Patty Mulville (p. 32); Patricia Perillo Norvet (pp. 44, 68); Dr. Harold Okone (pp. 19, 95); Phyllis Ottem, née Berger (p. 28); Ed Parsells (p. 59); Ann Perillo (p. 68); Carl Peterson (p. 73); Gloria Peterson (p. 73); Janet Peterson (p. 73); Lisa Peterson (p. 63); Ruth Carlson Peterson (p. 6); Joan Philosophos, née Johnson (p. 28); Joseph Plumpe (p. 15); Angela Pricoli, Anthony Pricoli, Sister Joan Pricoli, John Pricoli, John Pricoli Jr., Louisa Pricoli, Paul Pricoli, and Susan Pricoli (all p. 30); Marcia Rausch (p. 46); Judy Perillo San Gregorio (p. 63); Karin Sedgwick (p. 74); Josephine Fontaine Shea (p. 96); Donna Smith (p. 64); Louise Smith (p. 12); Nadine Spagnoli-Ganz (p. 23); Kerry

Jones Stich (p. 46); Ruth Edna Ogleve Stout (p. 43); Mr. and Mrs. Joe Taylor (p. 6); Amy Thomas (pp. 27, 108); Anne Thomas (pp. 27, 56, 108); Bill Thomas (p. 27); Mary Beth Thomas (pp. 27, 108); Mary Thomas (pp. 12, 20); Richard Thomas (pp. 20, 27); Steve Thomas (p. 108); Robert A. Thomas (p. 27); Jim Walsh (p. 20).

To Dorothy and Kitty (p. 81) and the others whose names have been lost to time, I hope my sincere thanks reach you, wherever you are.

EPHEMERA PHOTO CREDITS AND PERMISSIONS

Photographs on pages 8, 10, 25, 29, 34, 37, 42, 45, 57, 66, 67, 75, 88, 98, 100, 101, 104, 109, 111, 113, 116, 118, 125 by Paul D'Innocenzo. Items on pages 34, 45, 99, 111, and 125 appear courtesy of Pam Yosh (www.pamyosh.com). Thanks also to the proprietors of Alphaville in NYC and MIX in Edgartown, Massachusetts.

For their consultation and/or assistance with rights and permissions, I'm grateful to Christine Danuser, Rob Gretz, Larry Kass, Alissa Kleinman, Janis Manning, Michelle Massotti, Peter Peckham, Deborah Perantoni, Diane Scheid, Gretchen Testerman, and the helpful staffs of the New York Public Library; Science, Industry and Business Library; and Library and Archives Canada reference department, especially Line. Thanks to Professor Michelle Bogart of SUNY Stonybrook and to Daniel McCann of Illustration House, who enabled me to acknowledge the wonderful illustration of J. C. Leyendecker (p. 36).

page 14: Gretz Beer coaster appears with the permission of the Gretz Beer Company; page 37: The Smiley Logo is a registered Trademark of The Smiley Company SPRL—used with permission; page 40: Paul Jones advertisement is used with permission of Heaven Hill Distilleries, Inc.; page 55: SQUIRT is a registered trademark of A&W Concentrate Company. All rights reserved. Used with permission; page 85: Bell Telephone ad is reprinted with the permission of AT&T IP and Qwest; page 91: "Dig In and Dig Out the Scrap" poster from Library and Archives Canada, No. 1983-30-62, reproduction #C-087541.

DRINKS BY ALCOHOL

AMARETTO
Mother's Mai Tai 98
Nutty Candy 63

APPLE BRANDY
The All-American 52
Recycled Cup 90

APRICOT LIQUEUR
Demolition Daiquiri 74

**BECHEROVKA
(CZECH HERBAL LIQUEUR)**
Marvey Wall-Hanger 76

BEER
Señor Staycation (The Michelada) 106
Shandy Relations 14

BENEDICTINE & BRANDY
Auntie Dote 22

BLACKBERRY SCHNAPPS
Blackberry Curse 94

BLACK-CURRANT LIQUEUR
St. Kir 30

BOURBON
The All-American 52

BRANDY
Pink Slip-per Sangria 34
Sticker-Shock Sangria 89

CACHAÇA
Pet Peeve (strawberry caipirinha) 25

CAMPARI
Bittersweet Victory 70

**CHARTREUSE
(FRENCH HERBAL LIQUEUR)**
Green Daze 35

CHOCOLATE LIQUEUR
Nutty Candy 63

COFFEE LIQUEUR
Adulterated Coffee Break 37

DRAMBUIE
Fuzzy Date 21
Rusty Nail 67

ELDERFLOWER LIQUEUR
St. Kir 30

GIN
Astoria Iced Tea 102
En-gin Trouble 83
Naked Inhibition 101
Stand-Out Lemon-Lime Aid 105

GRAPPA
Cleaning Fluid 80

HARD CIDER
Recycled Cup 90

LILLET BLANC
Tour de Glass 97

OUZO
Astoria Iced Tea 102

PEACH SCHNAPPS
Fish-Story Punch 58
Fuzzy Date 21

PEAR BRANDY
Suspicious Package 110

PIMM'S NO. 1
Bug Zapper 62

POMEGRANATE LIQUEUR
Sandy Bathing Suit 109

RUM
Astoria Iced Tea 102
Demolition Daiquri 74
Fireman's Sour 88
Fish-Story Punch 58
Mother's Mai Tai 98
Name Your Poison 66
No Company Picnic 38
Security Blanket 18
Tour de Glass 97

RYE
Marathon Manhattan 48

SAKE
Propane Proxy 87

SCOTCH
Rusty Nail 67

SHERRY
Book-Club Buck 29

STRAWBERRY LIQUEUR
Name Your Poison 66

SOUR-APPLE LIQUEUR
Beach-House Bogart 17

TEQUILA
Silver Lining (frozen mango
    margarita) 75
Tech Tonic 41

TRIPLE SEC (ORANGE LIQUEUR)
Astoria Iced Tea 102
Auntie Dote 22
Mother's Mai Tai 98
Recycled Cup 90
Silver Lining (frozen mango
    margarita) 75

VERMOUTH
Dirty Ravaged Garden-tini 69
Cleaning Fluid 80
Marathon Manhattan 48
Naked Inhibition 101

VODKAS
Astoria Iced Tea 102
Decorator's Dream 72
Dirty Ravaged Garden-tini 69
Downturn Limoncello 61
The Handicap 45
Marvey Wall-Hanger 76
Muscle Relaxant 26
Sandy Bathing Suit 109

WHISKEY
Hole Punch 42
Theme-Park Prescription 55

WINE, STILL & SPARKLING
Auntie Dote (sparkling wine) 22
Holding Pattern (white wine) 84
Hole Punch (vinho verde) 42
Mom-osa (sparkling) 51
Pink Slip-per Sangria (rosé) 34
Sparkle Plenty (sparkling) 57
Sticker-Shock Sangria 89
St. Kir (sparkling) 30

RECIPES BY TYPE